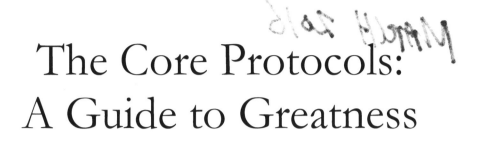

The Core Protocols:
A Guide to Greatness

Based on the work of
Jim McCarthy and Michele McCarthy

By Richard Kasperowski

With Great People

Nulogy

March 2016

The Core Protocols are copyright © Jim McCarthy and Michele McCarthy

This book and all additional material are copyright © 2014 Richard Kasperowski

All rights reserved. See License on page vii.

Version 1.2

ISBN: 0692381082
ISBN-13: 978-0692381083

CONTENTS

RICHARD KASPEROWSKI

FOREWORD

The more I study, practice, and share the Core Protocols, the more I recognize them as the single best way to get great results in all aspects of my life, and the more aligned I am with the vision of Jim and Michele McCarthy: All live in greatness.

I assembled the Core Protocols as a standalone book because I wanted to make them more accessible to the people I love so they can understand me better, so we can practice the Core together, and so we can reach for greatness together.

Thank you, Jim and Michele McCarthy, and everyone else who contributed to the Core Protocols. You are helping me reach for greatness.

-Richard Kasperowski

RICHARD KASPEROWSKI

LICENSE

The Core Protocols V. 3.03

Copyright (C) Jim McCarthy and Michele McCarthy

The Core is distributed under the terms of the GNU General Public License as published by the Free Software Foundation, either version 3 of the License, or (at your option) any later version. For exact terms see http://www.gnu.org/licenses/. The Core is considered as source code under that agreement. You are free to use and distribute this work or any derivations you care to make, provided you also distribute this source document in its entirety, including this paragraph.

The Core Protocols: A Guide to Greatness, based on the work of Jim McCarthy and Michele McCarthy

Copyright (C) Richard Kasperowski

This book is distributed under the terms of the GNU General Public License as published by the Free Software Foundation, either version 3 of the License, or (at your option) any later version. For exact terms see http://www.gnu.org/licenses/. This book is considered as source code under that agreement. You are free to use and distribute this work or any derivations you care to make, provided you also distribute this source document in its entirety, including this paragraph.

PART 1: HOW TO USE THIS BOOK

The purpose of this book is to share the Core Protocols more broadly. It is a concise summary of the Core Protocols in a small, bound printed book and as an ebook. You can read this guide to the Core Protocols on its own or in conjunction with Jim and Michele McCarthy's excellent book, *Software For Your Head*, 2001, Addison-Wesley, from which much of the material is pulled. For the Core Protocols, read both Part 2: The Core Commitments and Part 3: The Core Protocols.

This book also serves as a guide to a facilitated workshop. The purpose of the workshop is to help you and your team achieve greatness. The workshop lasts from a few hours to a couple of days; longer workshops achieve better results. The workshop is defined in the supplementary protocol, Workshop Express, defined in Part 4: Additional Information and Protocols. Part 4 also contains material from the *BootCamp Manual V2.3*, 2011, McCarthy Technologies, Inc., and from email correspondence with Jim McCarthy. To prepare for a workshop, or to learn more about the Core Protocols, read this book in its entirety.

To fully experience and embody the Core Protocols, attend a Core Protocols BootCamp. BootCamp is a multiday training session guaranteed to give your team the ability to design, implement, and deliver great products on time every time. To host or attend a BootCamp, find a certified Core Protocols BootCamp facilitator.

RICHARD KASPEROWSKI

The following Core Protocols are made up of both commitments and protocols.

PART 2: THE CORE COMMITMENTS*

1. I commit to engage when present.
    a. To know and disclose
        i. what I want,
        ii. what I think, and
        iii. what I feel.
    b. To always seek effective help.
    c. To decline to offer and refuse to accept incoherent emotional transmissions.
    d. When I have or hear a better idea than the currently prevailing idea, I will immediately either
        i. propose it for decisive acceptance or rejection, and/or
        ii. explicitly seek its improvement.
    e. I will personally support the best idea
        i. regardless of its source,
        ii. however much I hope an even better idea may later arise, and
        iii. when I have no superior alternative idea.
2. I will seek to perceive more than I seek to be perceived.
3. I will use teams, especially when undertaking difficult tasks.
4. I will speak always and only when I believe it will improve the general results/effort ratio.
5. I will offer and accept only rational, results-oriented behavior and communication.
6. I will disengage from less productive situations
    a. When I cannot keep these commitments,

The Core Commitments are the work of Jim McCarthy and Michele McCarthy.

      b. When it is more important that I engage elsewhere.

7. I will do now what must be done eventually and can effectively be done now.
8. I will seek to move forward toward a particular goal, by biasing my behavior toward action.
9. I will use the Core Protocols (or better) when applicable.
      a. I will offer and accept timely and proper use of the Protocol Check protocol without prejudice.
10. I will neither harm — nor tolerate the harming of — anyone for his or her fidelity to these commitments.
11. I will never do anything dumb on purpose.

PART 3: THE CORE PROTOCOLS†

Pass (Unpass)

The Pass protocol is how you decline to participate in something. Use it anytime you don't want to participate in an activity.

Steps

1. When you've decided not to participate, say, "I pass."
2. Unpass any time you desire. Unpass as soon as you know you want to participate again by saying, "I unpass."

Commitments

- Hold reasons for passing private.
- Pass on something as soon as you are aware you are going to pass.
- Respect the right of others to pass without explanation.
- Support those who pass by not discussing them or their pass.
- Do not judge, shame, hassle, interrogate or punish anyone who passes.

Notes

- In general, you will not be in good standing with your Core Commitments if you pass most of the time.
- You can pass on any activity; however, if you have adopted the Core Commitments, you cannot pass on a Decider vote and you must say "I'm in" when checking in.
- You can pass even though you have already started something.

---

† The Core Protocols are the work of Jim McCarthy and Michele McCarthy

Check In

Use Check In to begin meetings or anytime an individual or group Check In would add more value to the current team interactions.

Steps

1. Speaker says, "I feel [one or more of MAD, SAD, GLAD, AFRAID]." Speaker may provide a brief explanation. Or if others have already checked in, the speaker may say, "I pass." (See the Pass protocol.)
2. Speaker says, "I'm in." This signifies that Speaker intends to behave according to the Core Commitments.
3. Listeners respond, "Welcome."

Commitments

- State feelings without qualification.
- State feelings only as they pertain to yourself.
- Be silent during another's Check In.
- Do not refer to another's Check In disclosures without explicitly granted permission from him or her.

Notes

- In the context of the Core Protocols, all emotions are expressed through combinations of MAD, SAD, GLAD, or AFRAID. For example, "excited" may be a combination of GLAD and AFRAID.
- Check In as deeply as possible. Checking in with two or more emotions is the norm. The depth of a group's Check In translates directly to the quality of the group's results.
- Do not do anything to diminish your emotional state. Do not describe yourself as a "little" mad, sad, glad, or afraid, or say, "I'm mad, but I'm still glad."
- Except in large groups, if more than one person checks in, it is recommended that all do so.
- HAPPY may be substituted for GLAD, and SCARED may be substituted for AFRAID.

Check Out

Check Out requires that your physical presence always signifies your engagement. You must Check Out when you are aware that you cannot maintain the Core Commitments or whenever it would be better for you to be elsewhere.

Steps

1. Say, "I'm checking out."
2. Physically leave the group until you're ready to Check In once again.
3. Optionally, if it is known and relevant, you can say when you believe you'll return.
4. Those who are present for the Check Out may not follow the person, talk to or about the person checking out or otherwise chase him or her.

Commitments

- Return as soon as you can and are able to keep the Core Commitments.
- Return and Check In without unduly calling attention to your return.
- Do not judge, shame, hassle, interrogate, or punish anyone who checks out.

Notes

- When you Check Out, do it as calmly and gracefully as possible so as to cause minimal disruption to others.
- Check Out if your emotional state is hindering your success, if your receptivity to new information is too low, or if you do not know what you want.
- Check Out is an admission that you are unable to contribute at the present time.

Ask For Help

The Ask For Help protocol allows you to efficiently make use of the skills and knowledge of others.Ask For Help is the act that catalyzes connection and shared vision. Use it continuously, before and during the pursuit of any result.

Steps

1. Asker inquires of another, "[Helper's name], will you X?"
2. Asker expresses any specifics or restrictions of the request.
3. Helper responds by saying "Yes" or "No," or by offering an alternative form of help.

Commitments

- Always invoke the Ask For Help Protocol with the phrase "Will you . . ."
- Have a clear understanding of what you want from the Helper or if you do not have a clear understanding of what help you want, signal this by saying "I'm not sure what I need help with, but will you help me?"
- Assume that all Helpers are always available and trust that any Helper accepts the responsibility to say "No."
- Say "No" any time you do not want to help.
- Accept the answer "No" without any inquiry or emotional drama.
- Be receptive of the help offered.
- Offer your best help even if it is not what the asker is expecting.
- Postpone the help request if you are unable to fully engage.
- Request more information if you are unclear about the specifics of the help request.
- Do not apologize for asking for help.

Notes

- Asking for help is a low-cost undertaking. The worst possible outcome is a "No," which leaves you no further ahead or behind than when you asked. In the best possible outcome, you reduce the amount of time required to achieve a task and/or learn.
- Helpers should say "No" if they are not sure if they want to help. They should say nothing else after turning down a request for help.

8

- You cannot "over-ask" a given person for help unless he or she has asked you to respect a particular limit.

- If you don't understand the value of what is offered, or feel that it wouldn't be useful, or believe yourself to have considered and rejected the idea offered previously, assume a curious stance instead of executing a knee-jerk "But . . ." rejection. (See the Investigate protocol.)

- Asking in time of trouble means you waited too long to ask for help. Ask for help when you are doing well.

- Simply connecting with someone, even if he or she knows nothing of the subject you need help on can help you find answers within yourself, especially if you ask that person to Investigate you.

Protocol Check

Use Protocol Check when you believe a protocol is being used incorrectly in any way, or when a Core Commitment is being broken.

Steps

1. Say, "Protocol Check."
2. If you know the correct use of the protocol, state it. If you don't, ask for help.

Commitments

- Say "Protocol Check" as soon as you become aware of the incorrect use of a protocol, or of a broken Core Commitment. Do this regardless of the current activity.
- Be supportive of anyone using Protocol Check.
- Do not shame or punish anyone using Protocol Check.
- Ask for help as soon as you realize you are unsure of the correct protocol use.

Intention Check

Use Intention Check to clarify the purpose of your own or another's behavior. Use it when you aren't expecting a positive outcome resulting from the current behavior. Intention Check assesses the integrity of your own and another's intention in a given case.

Steps

1. Ask "What is your/my intention with X?" where X equals some type of actual or pending behavior to the person whose intention you want to know.
2. If it would be helpful, ask "What response or behavior did you want from whom as a result of X?"

Commitments

- Be aware of your own intention before checking the intention of another.
- Investigate sufficiently to uncover the intention of the person or his actions.
- Make sure you have the intention to resolve any possible conflict peacefully before intention-checking someone else. If you do not have a peaceful intention, Check Out.
- Do not be defensive when someone asks you what your intention is. If you can't do this, Check Out.

Notes

- If conflict arises that seems irresolvable, Check Out and Ask For Help.

Decider

Use Decider anytime you want to move a group immediately and unanimously towards results.

Steps

1. Proposer says, "I propose [concise, actionable behavior]."
2. Proposer says, "1-2-3."
3. Voters, using either Yes (thumbs up), No (thumbs down), or Support-it (flat hand), vote simultaneously with other voters.
4. Voters who absolutely cannot get in on the proposal declare themselves by saying, "I am an absolute no. I won't get in." If this occurs, the proposal is withdrawn.
5. Proposer counts the votes.
6. Proposer withdraws the proposal if a combination of outliers (No votes) and Support-it votes is too great or if proposer expects not to successfully conclude Resolution (below). You can approximate "too great" by using the following heuristics:
    a. approximately 50% (or greater) of votes are Support-it, OR
    b. the anticipated gain if the proposal passes is less than the likely cost of Resolution effort
7. Proposer uses the Resolution protocol with each outlier to bring him or her in by asking, "What will it take to get you in?"
8. Proposer declares the proposal carried if all outliers change their votes to Yes or Support-it.
9. The team is now committed to the proposed result.

Commitments

- Propose no more than one item per proposal.
- Remain present until the Decider protocol is complete; always remain aware of how your behavior either moves the group forward or slows it down.
- Give your full attention to a proposal over and above all other activity.
- Speak only when you are the proposer or are directed to speak by the proposer.
- Keep the reasons you voted as you did to yourself during the protocol.
- Reveal immediately when you are an absolute no voter and be ready to propose a better idea.

- Be personally accountable for achieving the results of a Decider commitment even if it was made in your absence.
- Keep informed about Decider commitments made in your absence.
- Do not argue with an absolute no voter. Always ask him or her for a better idea.
- Actively support the decisions reached.
- Use your capacity to "stop the show" by declaring you "won't get in no matter what" with great discretion and as infrequently as possible.
- Insist at all times that the Decider and Resolution protocols be followed exactly as per specification, regardless of how many times you find yourself doing the insisting.
- Do not pass during a Decider.
- Unceasingly work toward forward momentum; have a bias toward action.
- Do not look at how others are voting to choose your own vote.
- Avoid using Decider in large groups. Break up into small subgroups to make decisions, and use the large group to report status.

Notes

- Vote No only when you really believe the contribution to forward momentum you will make to the group after slowing or stopping it in the current vote will greatly outweigh the (usually considerable) costs you are adding by voting No.
- If you are unsure or confused by a proposal, support it and seek clarification offline after the proposal is resolved. If you have an alternate proposal after receiving more information, you can have faith that your team will support the best idea. (See "The Core Commitments")
- Voting No to make minor improvements to an otherwise acceptable proposal slows momentum and should be avoided. Instead, offer an additional proposal after the current one passes or, better yet, involve yourself in the implementation to make sure your idea gets in.
- Withdraw weak proposals. If a proposal receives less than seventy percent (approximately) Yes votes, it is a weak proposal and should be withdrawn by the proposer. This decision is, however, at the discretion of the proposer.
- Think of yourself as a potential solo outlier every time you vote

No.

- Vote Absolute No only when you are convinced you have a significant contribution to make to the direction or leadership of the group, or when integrity absolutely requires it of you.

Resolution

When a Decider vote yields a small minority of outliers, the proposer quickly leads the team, in a highly structured fashion, to deal with the outliers. The Resolution protocol promotes forward momentum by focusing on bringing outliers in at least cost.

Steps

1. Proposer asks outlier, "What will it take to get you in?"
2. Outlier states in a single, short, declarative sentence the precise modification required to be in.
3. Proposer offers to adopt the outlier's changes or withdraws the proposal.

Notes

- If the outlier's changes are simple, a simple Eye Check is performed to determine if everyone is still in.
- If the outlier's changes are complex, the proposer must withdraw the current proposal and then submit a new proposal that incorporates the outlier's changes.
- If the outlier begins to say why he voted No or to explain anything other than what it will take to get him or her in, the proposer must interrupt the outlier with, "What will it take to get you in?"

Perfection Game

The Perfection Game protocol will support you in your desire to aggregate the best ideas. Use it whenever you desire to improve something you've created.

Steps

1. Perfectee performs an act or presents an object for perfection, optionally saying "Begin" and "End" to notify the Perfector of the start and end of the performance.
2. Perfector rates the value of the performance or object on a scale of 1 to 10 based on how much value the Perfector believes he or she can add.
3. Perfector says, "What I liked about the performance or object was X," and proceeds to list the qualities of the object the Perfector thought were of high quality or should be amplified.
4. Perfector offers the improvements to the performance or object required for it to be rated a 10 by saying, "To make it a ten, you would have to do X."

Commitments

- Accept perfecting without argument.
- Give only positive comments: what you like and what it would take to "give it a 10."
- Abstain from mentioning what you don't like or being negative in other ways.
- Withhold points only if you can think of improvements.
- Use ratings that reflect a scale of improvement rather than a scale of how much you liked the object.
- If you cannot say something you liked about the object or specifically say how to make the object better, you must give it a 10.

Notes

- A rating of 10 means you are unable to add value, and a rating of 5 means you will specifically describe how to make the object at least twice as good.
- The important information to transmit in the Perfection Game protocol improves the performance or object. For example, "The

ideal sound of a finger snap for me is one that is crisp, has sufficient volume, and startles me somewhat. To get a 10, you would have to increase your crispness."

- As a perfectee, you may only ask questions to clarify or gather more information for improvement. If you disagree with the ideas given to you, simply don't include them.

Personal Alignment

The Personal Alignment protocol helps you penetrate deeply into your desires and find what's blocking you from getting what you want. Use it to discover, articulate, and achieve what you want. The quality of your alignment will be equal to the quality of your results.

Steps

1. Want: Answer the question, "What specifically do I want?"
2. Block: Ask yourself, "What is blocking me from having what I want?"
3. Virtue: Figure out what would remove this block by asking yourself "What virtue—if I had it—would shatter this block of mine?"
4. Shift: Pretend the virtue you identified is actually what you want.
5. Again: Repeat steps 2 to 4 until this process consistently yields a virtue that is powerful enough to shatter your blocks and get you what you originally thought you wanted.
6. Done: Now write down a personal alignment statement in the form "I want [virtue]." For example, "I want courage."
7. Signal/Response/Assignment: Create a signal to let others know when you are practicing your alignment, and provide a response they can give you to demonstrate support. For example, "When I say/do 'X,' will you say/do 'Y'?" Optionally, turn it into an assignment by saying you will do X a certain number of times per day, where X equals an activity that requires you to practice living your alignment.
8. Evidence: Write, in specific and measurable terms, the long-term evidence of practicing this alignment.
9. Help: Ask each member of your group for help. They help by giving the response you would like when you give your signal that you are practicing your alignment.

Commitments

*   Identify an alignment that will result in your personal change and require no change from any other person.
*   Identify blocks and wants that are specific and personal.
*   Identify blocks that, if solved, would radically increase your effectiveness in life, work, and play.
*   Choose a virtue that is about you and preferably one word long. For example: integrity, passion, self-care, peace, fun.

- Ask for help from people who know you and/or know alignments.
- Identify evidence that is measurable by an objective third party.

Notes

- The most popular personal alignments are, "I want (Integrity, Courage, Passion, Peace, Self-Awareness or Self-Care)."
- If you are struggling with figuring out what you want, adopt the alignment, "I want self-awareness." There is no case where increased self-awareness would not be beneficial.
- A personal block is something you find within yourself. It does not refer to circumstances or other people. Assume that you could have had what you want by now, that your block is a myth that somehow deprives you of your full potential.
- Ideally, identify both immediate and long-term evidence of your alignment. Write down results that start now (or very soon), as well as results you'll see at least five or more years in the future.
- As a default signal, tell your teammates or others who are close to you that you are working on your alignment when you are practicing it. If they don't know the protocol, just tell them what virtue you are working on and ask for their help.
- When members of a team are completing their personal alignments together (asking each other for help), the final step of the process is most powerful if done as a ceremony.

Investigate

Investigate allows you to learn about a phenomenon that occurs in someone else. Use it when an idea or behavior someone is presenting seems poor, confusing, or simply interesting.

Steps

1. Act as if you were a detached but fascinated inquirer, asking questions until your curiosity is satisfied or you no longer want to ask questions.

Commitments

- Ask well-formed questions.
- Ask only questions that will increase your understanding.
- Ask questions only if the subject is engaged and appears ready to answer more.
- Refrain from offering opinions.
- Do not ask leading questions where you think you know how he or she will answer.
- If you cannot remain a detached, curious investigator with no agenda, stop using the protocol until you can come back to it and keep these commitments.

Notes

- Do not theorize about the subject or provide any sort of diagnosis.
- Consider using the following forms for your questions:
  - o What about X makes you Y, Z?
  - o Would you explain a specific example?
  - o How does X go when it happens?
  - o What is the one thing you want most from solving X?
  - o What is the biggest problem you see regarding X now?
  - o What is the most important thing you could do right now to help you with X?
- Ineffective queries include the following:
  - o Questions that lead or reflect an agenda.
  - o Questions that attempt to hide an answer you believe is true.
  - o Questions that invite stories.
  - o Questions that begin with, "why."

- Stick to your intention of gathering more information.
- If you feel that you will explode if you can't say what's on your mind, you shouldn't speak at all. Consider checking your intention or Check Out.

PART 4: ADDITIONAL INFORMATION AND PROTOCOLS‡

Workshop Express

Use the Workshop Express protocol to facilitate and participate in a short workshop to guide a team through the Core Protocols. The purpose of the workshop is to make significant progress toward becoming great individuals and a great team. Because Team = Product, you will have significantly greater ability to achieve your goals, both individually and together.

Steps

1. One to two weeks prior to the workshop, the facilitator gives the host and attendees a copy of this book and an assignment. The assignment is to read and understand the contents of this book prior to attending the workshop, and, optionally, to read *Software for Your Head*.
2. Participants complete the assignment prior to the opening of the workshop.
3. The host and facilitator ensure that all participants have signed and returned a printed copy of the Personal Commitments Form.
4. The host opens the workshop by announcing the goal of the workshop. A typical stated goal is to build ourselves into a great team that always gets great results.
5. The facilitator states that the workshop is an "express" version of a Core Protocols BootCamp. The BootCamp is a five-day immersive experience that reliably transforms you and your team into a team that can design, implement, and deliver great products

‡ Workshop Express is the work of Richard Kasperowski. All other additional information and protocols in Part 4 are the work of Jim McCarthy and Michele McCarthy.

on time, every time. This express workshop is a shortened version of the BootCamp. We will use the Core Protocols and supplementary protocols to achieve a similar result in a much shorter amount of time. The workshop consists of these phases: i) introduce and review the Core Protocols, ii) understand and commit to supporting ourselves individually, iii) understand and commit to supporting each other, and iv) identify and articulate your Shared Vision together.

6. Introduce and review the Core Protocols
   a. The facilitator introduces the Core Protocols. The Core Protocols are a set of fundamental behaviors that, when practiced together, reproducibly help individuals and teams get great outcomes.
   b. The facilitator emphasizes the importance of the Pass protocol.
   c. The facilitator reads or recites the Core Commitments.
   d. The facilitator and participants Check In.
   e. The facilitator emphasizes the importance of the Ask For Help protocol. The facilitator passively participates in the rest of the workshop, offering help only when explicitly asked.
   f. The facilitator explains the Protocol Check protocol. During the rest of the workshop, participants use Protocol Check, Ask For Help, and other protocols to ensure they understand the Core Protocols and practice them correctly, and to make progress toward their goal.

7. Be a great self—understand and commit to supporting ourselves individually. The participants use Personal Alignment Express and other protocols to discover and articulate what they want individually.

8. Be a great team—understand and commit to supporting each other: The participants use Web of Commitment Express and other protocols to align as a team and to celebrate their alignment.

9. Get great results—identify and articulate your Shared Vision together. The participants use Decider Protocol, Perfection Game, and other protocols to align on and articulate their Shared Vision.

10. Celebrate!

Commitments

- Give Jim and Michele McCarthy full credit for the Core Commitments, the Core Protocols, and all following Additional Information and Protocols.

- The facilitator must Booted; that is, the facilitator must have attended one or more full Core Protocols BootCamps.
- This workshop is not a full BootCamp. Only a McCarthy certified Core Protocols BootCamp facilitator may conduct a Core Protocols BootCamp.

Notes

- When you complete your Personal Alignment Express, Web of Commitment Express, and align on and articulate your Shared Vision, you are a great team, ready to accomplish great things!
- Small groups—five people or fewer—work best as you align on your Shared Vision.

Personal Commitments

Please initial each commitment and sign at the bottom, indicating you agree to the following:

1. Safety. I will take care of myself, my privacy and my safety during this course. I know that I can Pass on anything and Check Out at will, with no penalties attached.
Initials _____

2. Staff. I want to learn about myself, about team dynamics, about my teammates, and I want to understand what the course staff understands about teams. For the duration of the course, I will suspend disbelief and adopt as a learning strategy the pretense that presented ideas are true. I want to learn efficiently and I am willing to accept the staff's guidance to find new efficiency in my learning. I will refrain from providing feedback during the course.
Initials _____

3. The Core Culture. I have read The Core Commitments and Protocols to be used in the course. I agree to adhere to The Core Commitments and Protocols during the course. This includes requiring that others on my team adhere to The Core Protocols and Commitments.
Initials _____

4. Durability. If any of the above (1–3) commitments are untrue of me now or become untrue sometime during the course, I will resolve this with the staff immediately.
Initials _____

Name _____ Date _____

Personal Alignment Express

Like the Personal Alignment protocol, Personal Alignment Express helps you penetrate deeply into your desires and find what's blocking you from getting what you want. Use it to discover, articulate, and achieve what you want. The quality of your alignment will be equal to the quality of your results.

Total time to complete this is about 1 hour, 30 minutes.

Note: To successfully complete this task, you must be willing to be vulnerable. The more vulnerable you are, the greater your results will be. If you prefer not to be vulnerable, or don't care to do this work for any reason, Pass or Check Out (see Core Protocols) and quietly leave or do something else. Also note that defaults are provided to save time in most steps.

Steps

Part One

(Alone, do steps 1–6: 30 minutes)

1. What do you WANT?
    a. What BLOCKS you from having what you WANT?
    b. What VIRTUE would dissolve that BLOCK? Pick one.
        • Self-Awareness (default; if you don't know what you want, you want self-awareness)
        • Integrity
        • Courage
        • Passion
        • Peace
        • Presence
        • Self-Care
        • Fun
        • Wisdom
        • Health

(Note: In choosing a virtue, imagine that you will soon master it. Pretend that wanting it will summon it. For example, if you choose passion, passion will be ever-present to you. You will master passion. You will know all about it. You will attain the perfect amount of passion for your own life.

You will be a model and a teacher for others when it comes to passion. You might compose the standard protocols and practices for passion, etc., etc. You will enjoy the fruits of a passionate life.)

2. Optionally, to go deeper:
   a. Shift VIRTUE to WANT (i.e., "VIRTUE X is now what I WANT").
   b. Go back to step 1a with that new WANT.
   c. Iterate 1a-1d until: 1) you find the virtue that would dissolve the final block you are aware of; or 2) you don't feel like iterating anymore.
3. My ALIGNMENT: I want _____.
   Write the VIRTUE as your alignment.
4. My SIGNAL:
   What I will say and/or do to signal that a) I am about to practice my Alignment, or b) I am about to report on my Alignment work, or c) I am celebrating my Alignment:
   Default: "I am practicing my Alignment: virtue-name."
5. The RESPONSE I want from others when I so signal:
   What I ask my teammates to say and/or do in response when I signal; how they can support me in my Alignment work, my new behavior
   Default: "When I say signal, will you respond by expressing support, and, if I want it, by making a little time for me in the moment?"
6. Some observable EVIDENCE that will exist in the world after I have attained—or as I practice—my Alignment.
   Changes or accomplishments other people will be able to observe. Evidence, as in a court of law.
   Default: "I will be able to show a report card I get from (named people) every (interval) on my progress with respect to Alignment."

Part Two

(Pairs, or triples: do steps 7–8: 60 minutes)

7. Pair up or triple up with teammates, preferably those whom you don't know very well, but would like to know better. Now spend an hour Investigating (see Core Protocols) each other's wants, blocks and Alignment. If you like, spend the time trading off in ten- or fifteen-minute chunks. Don't be afraid to change your alignment. You can also break off and join others, staying in Investigate-mode, if time remains and it seems right. Be vulnerable,

be curious.

8. Decide on your final Alignment.

Web of Commitment Express

NOTE: Sincerity, depth, passion and vulnerability are essential. The more of each from all, the greater the team's ultimate results will be.

Steps

1. Create a ritual space.
2. Team proceeds in silence into the ritual space.
3. Each member of the team, in turn, as desired:
    a. Says: "I want Alignment-virtue."
    b. Offers: From the heart, any key sentiments/thoughts/ feelings describing the Alignment choice.
    c. Asks for Help:
       Ask each teammate, one at a time:

       "When I signal, will you response?"

       AND/OR

       Asks for help anticipated in the future with respect to Alignment.

    d. When each team member has done a–c, and all team members have closure on all help requests, the Web of Commitment is in place.
4. To exercise the Web, each team member accepts the following assignment:
    At least one time during the course, or after, but while still with some teammates, or even in email after that, you will inform the team you are working on your Alignment by saying your signal.

Shared Vision

Don't do any work on the assignment until you have a Shared Vision. You will need to learn Check In, Decider and Personal Alignment to get your Shared Vision. Then your work will proceed in the direction of greatness. Personal Alignment will probably take the highest percentage of the BootCamp time. This is OK. Successful completion of Personal Alignment and Shared Vision will guarantee that your team is maximally productive while in what we are used to calling the "development" phase of your project, but which is actually just the final stage of development.

State of Shared Vision

Shared Vision is the state of being that your team is in once everyone is Aligned and has completed the Web of Commitment. Being in a state of Shared Vision is evident by how the team is practicing their Alignments, trusting instead of controlling, and doing instead of discussing. When you have achieved Shared Vision, you will find people on your team will exchange ideas more quickly and two separate works will align when brought together. You will notice that you are "seeing as one."

Shared Vision Statement = Far Vision Statement

The Far Vision Statement is a statement that describes the world your team will build. It is one of the things your team produces while in the state of Shared Vision.

Far Vision is a term we use to differentiate between Near and Far when creating visions. Once you have a Far Vision you can start creating visions in the near term that describe steps you will take to reach the far vision. Those are the Versions of your product.

Get Help With the Shared Vision Protocols

(Get help at every point. It is common to stop asking for help once the Web of Commitment is complete as if no more help would help.)

First, make sure your Web of Commitment is actually complete before you move on. Ask the Consultants for help on the quality of your team's Web of Commitment to determine when it is effective to move on.

Use Decider Protocol and Perfection Game to help you get into a state of Shared Vision and to help you create a Far Vision Statement that:

- Is very short and to the point (fewer than ten words).

- Gives the reader a picture of how the world will be different when you are done. For example, "A Computer on Every Desk" or "A Man on the Moon."
- Is catchy, hits the reader in the gut, and addresses some desire of the reader. The reader says, "Yes!" when he sees it and realizes that it is something he wants. For example, "A Wireless World."

There will likely be some fighting around doing this as part of the Shared Vision Recoil. Once your team has a Shared Vision, it is recommended that a few people work on the statement while others begin work on the product.

Creating a Far Vision

- After having completed Alignment with your team, write a statement which best expresses for all of you what the world will look like when your work together is done. Use Decider Protocol and Perfection Game as your primary tools.
  - o The Far Vision should be comprised of words. It cannot be a symbol or song, etc.
  - o The Far Vision must be imaginative. Look as far into the future as possible. Twenty years is a good starting point, but it must be beyond your ability to extrapolate current trends. That is, it must be the work of intention and imagination, not analysis.
  - o The Far Vision must be measurable. Ideally, progress can be measured as well. The desired result may be something readily measurable: an observable, external thing or event—for example, "Put a man on the moon." Or it might be softer and harder to measure, such as, "Create infinite, free bandwidth." Your Far Vision could also be values-driven—harder, but still possible to measure—such as, "Eliminate Poverty," or "Ubiquitous Radical Democracy."
  - o The Far Vision Statement should just be a few words, ideally no more than ten. If it is more than six words, ask your team to reevaluate it.
  - o The Far Vision should be catchy or engage the listener. (It should invoke a visceral response.) It is a marketing message to the rest of the world about how the world will be different because of your team's work.
  - o The team should unanimously support the Far Vision, using Decider.

- Now form a product vision—a vision statement for the first Version. This statement should follow the same guidelines as the Far Vision Statement. The Version statement should describe the most important thing the team can do now to move the world furthest toward the world in their Far Vision.
- The Far Vision and Version statements are the raw materials for creating messages within and outside the team. Therefore, clarity and vividness are the most important characteristics for a statement of this type. Convey all that is necessary with as few words as possible, in an easily understood, memorable phrase.

Examples of Far Vision Statements and Version Statements

- Put a man on the moon.
  o Version 1: Orbit the Earth
- A computer on every desk.
  o Version 1: A computer on every desk in our company.
- World peace.
  o Version 1: Peace in our family.
- A world without wires.
  o Version 1: Cell phones instead of desk phones for our team.

Complete Your Shared Vision

Don't work on or agree to work on a product until your Shared Vision is complete (which means all Alignment and Web of Commitment work is done).

Your Managers will not be happy with anything less than your team having a Shared Vision. That is why they hired the McCarthy Technologies, Inc. staff to help you. So don't promise or do anything less, even if you think it will meet your Managers' needs in the short term.

In the first Manager meeting they will ask you if you have been maximizing your use of the Consultants, and if you understand and follow their advice. If you haven't, you will feel like you have wasted some time, because your Managers will insist you take full advantage of all your resources for this project.

Remember:

- Your Managers will most likely catch you in anything short of the truth.
- Your Managers will be able to tell when you don't have a Shared Vision.

- Your Managers will always know when you didn't Ask for Help.
- Your Managers will always know when you are acting like you know something you don't know.
- Your Managers will get tougher when you get defensive, and they will relax when you tell the truth and are receptive.

Take Advantage of the Benefits of Your State of Shared Vision

As part of post-Shared Vision Recoil, the team will backslide into old habits of work. These are habits designed to cope with a world where there are few Shared Visions. These habits might include:

- Not trusting that others' work will be OK if they work apart from your view. Not wanting to split up into smaller groups.
- Wanting to implement some particular process scheme.
- Wanting to "brainstorm" instead of follow the intuition of the team towards the deliverables.

In BootCamp world, once you have a Shared Vision you can drop many of the habits you have developed to control things at work. After achieving Shared Vision, we recommend doing the following:

- Split up into sub-teams. Your work will match up well because you can stay connected with each other and you share the same vision.
- Just talk about cool ideas as they occur. You don't have to control the discussion with a brainstorming session.
- Follow the visionaries. Some people on the team will undoubtedly have visions for product pieces. Just start implementing those. There is no downside to making something while your team is in a state of Shared Vision.
- Make sure someone understands the business case of your course. How does your course translate into dollars?
- Use what you know about processes to get results on your deliverables, but don't have a discussion about process itself or spend the team's energy trying to get support for a process.
- Start making things. You will find your way by creating the product. "Planning" is generally a bad idea.
- Keep making sure all the "scary" ideas are out. Has everyone on your team exhausted his creative resources? 9 times out of 10, someone is not saying a great idea because of some type of fear.
- Wait for the big idea. If the ideas seem to cause a lot of effort or work wait and relax awhile. It is likely there is a bigger idea that will solve a bunch of problems and take less effort.

- Use the Perfection Game repeatedly in sub-teams. Using the Perfection Game in a large group is too time-consuming for the results attained.

ABOUT THE AUTHOR

 **Richard Kasperowski** pursues a vision that all software developers and teams are great. He works as a Business Transformation Coach, Agile Coach, and Open Space Facilitator, helping people, teams, and organizations understand what they have, discover and align around what they want, and transform from what they have to what they want. As a coach, manager, and team member, he has worked with some of the largest (and smallest) technology companies in the world, helping them get better outcomes.

Follow Richard on Twitter at @rkasper, read more about him at www.kasperowski.com, and email him at richard@kasperowski.com.

25346353R00028

Made in the USA
Middletown, DE
27 October 2015